LEARNING CENTOS 7

A BEGINNERS GUIDE TO USING LINUX

NATHAN JAMES NEIL

Copyright © 2016

See More Books by Nathan Neil:

NeilPublishing.com

"In real open source, you have the right to control your own destiny."

- Linus Torvalds

Table of Contents

Chapter 1 6
    What is Linux & CentOS? 6
    Methods to Install CentOS 7 & Getting Started 8
    Quick Recap 10

Chapter 2 11
    Installing CentOS on a VPS 11
    Setting Up CentOS on Linode 12
    Setting Up CentOS on Digital Ocean 15

Chapter 3 19
Installing CentOS onto a Virtual Machine 19
    Installing Oracle VirtualBox 19
    Getting The ISO 24
    Configuring and Installing CentOS To Oracle VirtualBox .. 25
        CentOS 7 Installation 27

Chapter 4 33
60 Second Documentation Bootcamp 33

Chapter 5 35
    Getting to the CLI 35
    Logging In for the First Time 37
    Navigation 38
    Quick Recap 42

Chapter 6 43
    Creating a New User 43
    Quick Recap 46

Chapter 7 47

    System Status at a Glance 47

    Navigating, Making Directories, and Files 49

        Creating and Editing Files With Nano 52

        Editing, Deleting, Moving, and Copying 56

Chapter 8 60

    Updating The Server 60

Chapter 9 62

    Setting Up a Web Server 62

        Apache2 62

        The Web Folder 64

        Installing MySQL/MariaDB Database 65

        Installing PHP5 66

        Installing Sendmail 67

Chapter 10 69

    Management Via The Browser 69

Chapter 11 71

    Understanding Permissions 71

        Permission Groups 72

        Permission Types 72

        Using Binary References to Set Permissions 73

        Overview: Ownership of Files and Directories 75

Chapter 12 77

    Adding a Database to MariaDB 77

Chapter 13 79

Preparing For And Installing WordPress 79

Downloading Wordpress 80

Recap on Changing Ownership and Permissions And Editing Files 82

Accessing WordPress Via The Browser 84

Chapter 14 86

Final Remarks 86

Chapter 1

What is Linux & CentOS?

You may be familiar with Microsoft Window's and Apple's MacOSX. Both of these are examples of operating systems and so is Linux.

Merriam-Webster defines **operating system** as the main program in a computer that controls the way the computer works and makes it possible for other programs to function.

Essentially, the operating system is the program that lets you interact with a computer, and the computer to understand what you want to do. Operating systems are required for computers to work, but in our interconnected world, they are also used in smart phones, cars, home appliances, and basically everything. With no operating system our devices are just hunks of plastic, glass, and silicone.

Linux is an open-source operating system. Being open-source is a major difference between Linux and the other popular operating systems. **Open-source** means that the software is provided with the original source code and is made freely available to be redistributed and modified. This is what makes Linux unique. It has a strong community out there modifying the code, participating in forums, and fixing bugs much quicker than the alternatives.

If you are looking to add a new skill to your portfolio, learning how to use Linux, can be very useful. According to ZDNet in 2014, 87% of enterprise businesses added at least one Linux server and 82% planned on adding more in 2015.

Linux and its distributions are very popular for database, web, and other types of servers. Being around since the 90's, Linux powers most of the internet, supercomputers that enable breakthroughs in science, and the stock exchanges of the globe. As you look at the internet, Linux powers over 36% of the resources online, of that about 21% is the CentOS Linux distribution.

A **distro** or **distribution** is a version or 'flavor' of Linux that uses the Linux kernel as its foundation. The kernel is the one component that is actually called Linux. The **kernel** is the lowest level of the operating system and manages the primary system functions for the CPU, memory, and devices.

In 1991, a personal project by Linus Torvalds was to create a new free operating system kernel. Since then the kernal has been marked with constant growth over the last 25 years. It has grown from a small number of C based files to over 18 million lines of xource code that is open under the GNU General Public Licence.

There are hundreds of Linux distros and most are free to use, but just three distros dominate the infrastructure of the internet: Ubuntu, Debian, and CentOS. CentOS is a distribution of Linux, which is derived from the sources of Red Hat Enterprise Linux. It is noted for being incredibly stable, predictable, and managable. Since 2004 CentOS Linux has been community-supported and free to use. From CentOS and its community, you can get a fantastic operating system to manage websites, databases, and run other services, while also getting support from a growing community. Almost a quarter of servers running Linux, are using CentOS.

There are a lot of distributions out there and some differences between them. I personally started in an Ubuntu enviroment when I began learning and consider the functionality between the two comparable, but with strong differences in some of their user interaction. CentOS is becoming more of a standard for those who want to host sites and utilize products like cPanel and other hosting software tools. They have been standardizing on CentOS due to its slower release cycle. This book will explore using CentOS, and in the process teach general Linux usage.

METHODS TO INSTALL CENTOS 7 & GETTING STARTED

The tools that you will need, vary on the route that you would like to go. There are four installation methods, that you could use to experiment with the lessons in this book.

Methods for Installing an OS for Experimentation

1. Use a Low Cost Cloud Virtual Private Server (VPS)
2. Install the OS Using Virtualization Software
3. Install the OS onto a Computer
4. Dual Boot Your Existing Computer

We will explore the first two of these options in this book. When I started writing books about Linux, one of my first books was: Learning Ubuntu. The book is ranked as one of the top books for Learning Ubuntu and managing Linux in that enviroment, but I did receive one critisim. A few people did not like that my recommendation was to use a service that cost money (VPS) and wanted other solutions for learning. My motto is that knowledge is worth sharing, but installing the OS onto a machine, especially one that you rely on is risky. To provide more detail, we will review two VPS services and also how to install CentOS on your computer using virtualization software (Oracle VirtualBox).

If you want to use options 3 or 4, you can find a lot of tutorials on YouTube that you can reference. I strongly recommend against trying to install it yourself if you are new to the field and would recommend getting familier with the other options outlined in this book first. Options 1 & 2 are the safest and most effective way to get started quickly.

Before we talk about these methods to get started, lets first go over the version of CentOS that we will be using for this book. This book, while it can apply to other versions of CentOS, is best suited for CentOS 7. One of the main reasons that CentOS is becoming popular is that their OS is supported for ten years from release, while many others only have five year support cycles. CentOS 7 was release in 2014 and has support until 2024. Many people do not realize that an operating system's support expires.

Once the support expires, there may not be security patches and other upgrades for it available.

In my book, [Securing Business Data: Establishing a Core Value for Data Security](), we talk about operating system support more in depth. If you work with technology or manage a business, I highly recommend that you read it.

CentOS is supported by nearly all VPS providers. VPS stands for Virtual Private Server. A **Virtual Private Server** is a machine sold as a hosting service and is often more affordable than purchasing a server and the bandwidth that it requires. With the popularity of cloud based services, many businesses now run more virtual private servers in order to conserve costs and scale more quickly. With a VPS you pay for what you need to use and can add more resources overtime, if you find you need more processing power or memory.

Quick Recap

1) An **operating system** is the main program in a computer, which controls the way the computer works, making it possible for other programs to function.
    a. Microsoft Windows, Mac OSX, and Linux are examples of operating systems.
2) **Open-source** means that the software is provided with the original source code and is made freely available to be redistributed and modified.
3) A **distro** or **distribution** is a version of Linux that uses the Linux kernel as its foundation.
4) A **Virtual Private Server** is a machine sold as a hosting service and is often more affordable than purchasing a server and the bandwidth that it requires
5) The recommend method for you to experiment with CentOS, is by setting up a VPS.
    a. This books instructions focus on using DigitalOcean or Linode as your host, but you can choose other providers as well.

Chapter 2

Installing CentOS on a VPS

In this section of the book, we will cover the installation method of using a Virtual Private Server.

A **VPS** is a virtual machine sold as a service by an internet hosting service. It runs its own OS and customers are provided super user access to the operating system. This allows users to install and manage almost anything they wish for their operating system.

A few other advantages to a VPS is that you can access it from anywhere. It is hosted in the cloud and if you want to use CentOS to host a website, it provides a great way to get started without needing your own high tier of internet bandwidth and appropriate hardware. Personally, this is what I use for my websites. It is cheaper than buying the internet connection for a fast web experience and hardware to run a robust server out of the house.

In this section we will cover getting started with two VPS providers: Linode and DigitalOcean. Each has their own pricing and service offerings, but both are easy to start with.

When you are choosing a VPS provider there are several things to consider. Since you are getting started and learning, price is likely to be a major part of your decision if you choose this method. On Linode, they offer a 1GB memory, 1CPU, 24GB storage, and 2 TB transfer server for $10 per month. DigitalOcean has a starter package with 512MB memory, 1 CPU, 20GB storage, and 1 TB transfer for

$5 per month. The choice is up to you. DigitalOcean also has a $10 plan similar to the starting plan on Linode.

SETTING UP CENTOS ON LINODE

To get started with a Virtual Private Server or VPS is very simple. All you need is a credit card and this book! You can get your server live in just a few minutes.

First you will need to go to: https://www.linode.com/

From there you can sign up and select which plan you would like. For me making this guide with intentions to launch a small eCommerce site, I am going to start with the $10 plan.

After you select the plan, you need to select the datacenter you wish to use. My recommendation is to choose one that is the closest to your location.

Location
Newark, NJ

[Add this Linode!]

I am located in Pennsylvania so Newark, NJ is the closest datacenter. I select that and then click 'Add this Linode'.

Once you do this, you will now be brought to the Linode Manager. This is a location where you can manage all of your VPS systems, if you have multiple.

Linodes	NodeBalancers	Longview	DNS Manager	Account	Support

Linodes

Linode	Status	Plan	IP	Location
linode1938051	Being Created	Linode 1024	45.33.83.194	Newark, NJ, USA

The image above may be hard to see, but from here we can see the status of our Linode, the Plan we are using, and our IP address. That number for the IP address is what we will use to connect to our server and eventually connect our domain to. It is very important so it might not be a bad idea to write it down.

Right now, the server is empty with no operating system. We need to install onto it the OS we wish to use, which for this book is CentOS 7.

Click on the name of your Linode. In this instance the name is linode1938051. Yours will appear similar to that.

When you click on the name, you will notice that it looks rather empty. Again it is because we need to install the OS.

VPS providers make this very easy. On Linode, we simply need to click the deploy link.

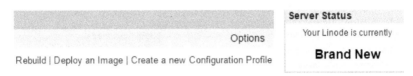

Click on 'Deploy an Image'.

From this window, we can select the Image we want, which is CentOS 7. Leave the defaults for now in the deployment disk size and swap disk. Enter in what you would like the password to be for root (will be discussed more later) and make sure that it is a secure password. Once all of this is done click on the 'Deploy' button.

Once you click 'Deploy' the system will start the installation. Give this a few moments to complete, but for now your installation work is done! If you choose to use Linode, then you can skip the next section on the alternative, DigitalOcean. Please note that there are more providers than just these two, but these are my personal preference for beginners.

SETTING UP CENTOS ON DIGITAL OCEAN

Like Linode, DigitalOcean offers a quick process to get started and deploy a CentOS installation. If you have decided to pay the small monthly fee for a VPS with any provider, I think you made the right decision. What I like about using a VPS is that it doesn't use my machines hardware and I can work on it from anywhere that I have an internet connection.

Let's go ahead and get our server setup with DigitalOcean in just a few minutes.

First, go to https://www.digitalocean.com/ and click on 'Sign Up' in the top right. From there, enter an email address and password that you want to use for your account. Then click 'Sign Up'.

Now we need to confirm our email address. Open your email and find the email from DigitalOcean. It will be titled "DigitalOcean – Please confirm your email address." Open the email and proceed to click on the verification link.

Great, now that our email is confirmed, we need to select a payment option. DigitalOcean gives you the option of using a credit card or PayPal. For me, I use PayPal for convenience.

If you use PayPal, you have to prepay $5, which is credited to your account. This will cover our first month!

Once you have added your payment method, we can create our VPS, what DigitalOcean calls a Droplet. In the top right, click on the green 'Create Droplet' button.

Next, it will ask you to select a distribution. We want to select CentOS and the most recent edition they offer, which is 7.2.

Once you have selected CentOS, scroll down to select the size of server you want to deploy. They have the $20 per month plan selected as the default. Just click on the $5 per month plan, if that is the size you would like to use to get started.

Choose a size

I recommend selecting a region based on your location. Since I am in the USA on the east coast, New York is my pick for this provider.

Choose a datacenter region

Under the additional options, it is up to you if you would like a backup. If we were doing development or anything outside of training and testing, I would recommend selecting the backup option, but since we just want the basics for now to learn, I am going to leave these options unchecked.

From there, scroll down to the bottom and click the big green 'Create' button.

Then in a matter of a few seconds, your system is setup and ready. DigitalOcean will then email you the IP address, username, and password for your server. Keep this information handy. We will need the IP address and login information shortly.

Chapter 3
Installing CentOS onto a Virtual Machine

If you do not wish to use a VPS yet and want to work locally with your testing, then the next best choice is to use a Virtual Environment. Many of them are on the market. I would recommend this for two reasons. It is less risky than installing on a machine you use and if you have a fairly decent computer, it doesn't really cost anything to get started. Assuming that you are a beginner and just getting started, we will start from scratch and install the virtualization software first. Oracle's VirtualBox, which is the program we will use for this tutorial, is open source and free.

Installing Oracle VirtualBox

In this demo, I will be using a x64 Windows 10 computer.

To install VirtualBox go to:
https://www.virtualbox.org/wiki/Downloads

From there select which version best fits your system. For me using a Windows 10 x64 machine, I am going to download **VirtualBox 5.0.20 for Windows hosts**.

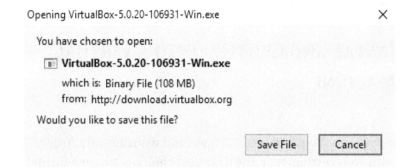

When you click the link to download and are prompted, click Save File. Once it has downloaded, click the executable to start the installation.

When prompted click 'Next'.

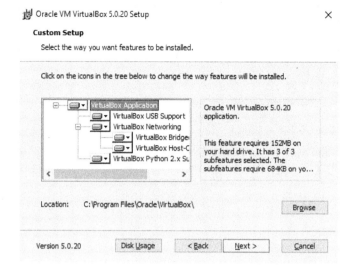

Leave the settings as the default and click 'Next' again.

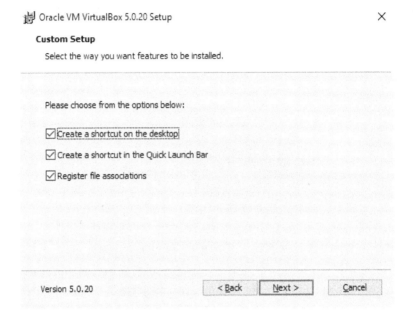

If you want the shortcuts, which can be useful, leave the default settings and click 'Next' once more. Now we are done clicking 'Next'. ☺

The following prompt, will alert you that installing the Oracle Virtual Box Networking feature will reset your network connection and temporarily disconnect you from the internet. This is ok and you can click 'Yes' to continue.

Once you have clicked 'Yes', you will be at the final installation prompt as depicted below. Click the default 'Install' button.

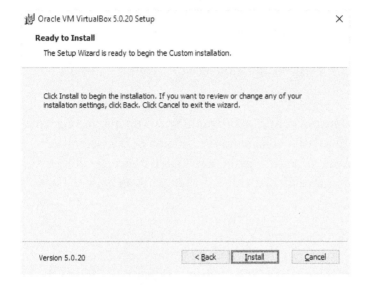

Now we wait. It isn't as long as the wait for winter to come in the popular book and television series Game of Thrones, but it will take a few moments.

As the installer proceeds, you may need to click 'Yes' or 'Install' another time or two. When it is completed you will see a completion screen. Click on 'Finish' and it will launch VirtualBox.

Getting The ISO

To either install CentOS using VirtualBox or to set it up on your own, you will need to download the operating systems iso file. An **iso** is the file extension used for files that can be burned to a CD or DVD, depending on the size. Essentially it is an image of the installation disc that you will need to install CentOS.

For us to install CentOS to VirtualBox, we do not need to burn the ISO to a DVD and can mount it inside of the virtual enviroment. If you are looking to install it directly onto a machine or attempt a dual boot, then you will need to burn this file.

To get the most recent ISO file for CentOS, go to https://www.centos.org/ and click "Get CentOS". I personally downloaded the Minimal ISO and recommend that for you to get started using the system and the tutorials in this book.

There are multiple locations or mirrors to download the iso from. Choose one and download the CentOS 7 operating system ISO.

Once you download the iso file, if you are not using VirtualBox, you will need to burn it to a disc. There are a variety of iso burning tools. In the past, I have used Ashampoo Burning Studio Free, with success.

If you are going to use VirtualBox, then follow the steps to mount the ISO and setup your virtual machine in the next section.

Configuring and Installing CentOS To Oracle VirtualBox

Now that we have downloaded the ISO and have Oracle VirtualBox installed, we can setup our virtual enviroment. Launch VirtualBox and click the "New" button so that we can configure a virtual machine to run CentOS.

Once you click "New", we need to name the machine and provide some basic information. See the image below as a guide. Remember that CentOS is based on the Red Hat Enviroment.

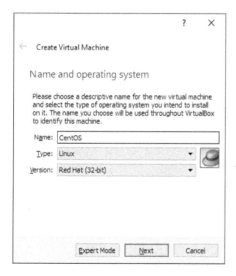

Once that is completed, click "Next". The software will recommend the amound of memory to allocate to your virtual machine. I would personally allocate 1GB of memory or 1024MB at a minimum. When that is finalized, click next and then select "Create a Virtual Hard Disk". Click create to allocate the virtual hard disk to the machine.

Afterwards it will ask you for your preferred format. I personally stick with the VDI format, which is the default. Once that is selected, the next prompt askes if you would like a dynamic disk that only uses disk space as it is used by the virtual machine. A fixed disk will automatically use the full space of the allocated disk on your machine. My preference is the dynamically allocated option.

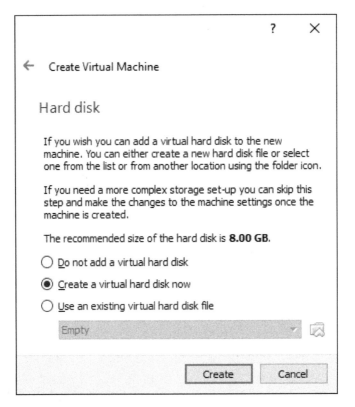

Once you have completed the wizard, you will need to mount the ISO to the virtual DVD drive. Basically this is the same as entering the installation media (DVD in this case) into a physical machine. In VirtualBox click "Settings", then "Storage", and then click "Add Optical Drive".

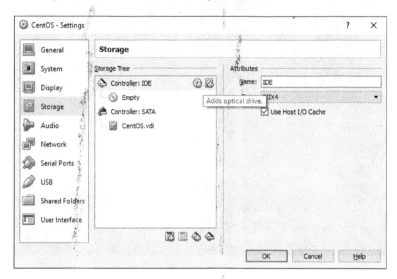

Select the ISO file and click ok. Now back at the main menu click "Start".

The virtual machine will begin to start.

CENTOS 7 INSTALLATION

Once the machine boots, you will see the screen below.

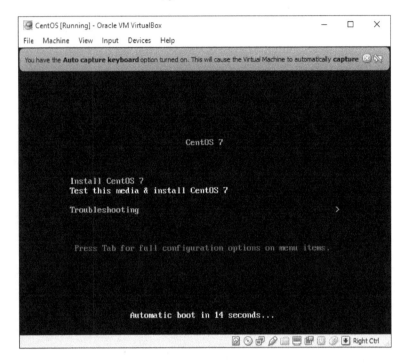

Select Install CentOS 7 and press enter.

If your installation fails or appears to hang, it is likely that your system does not support running 64bit software virtually. I experienced that issue as I was testing for this book on an older PC.

You can download the 32bit i386 versions from this link: http://mirror.centos.org/altarch/7/isos/i386/

Once the installer successfully loads, you will need to select your language and location. Once you have done that click "Continue".

Next you will see CentOS preconfigure a variety of settings.

You may need to configure the "Installation Destination" that is under the system heading. Select "Installation Destination" and from that interface select the hard disk and click done as seen below.

Once that is complete and you are back at the main installation screen. Now we need to make sure that we can establish an internet connection. Click on "Network and Hostname". Inside of this panel configure and make sure that "Automatically Connect When Network is Available" is checked. Once that is completed, click save. In the hostname box, enter the name for your server. I just called mine centOS. When that is completed turn the switch for the network adapter to on. It can be found right next to the network adapter. In the top left click, "Done", which returns you to the home screen where you can click "Begin Installation" in the bottom right.

As CentOS is installing there are two things we can configure, the "Root Password" and "User Creation". For now lets leave the user configuration the way it is and set the "Root Password". Click on "Root Password", enter the new password twice and then click done. Be sure to remember this password as we will need it later.

Once the installation is completed, you will need to click the "Reboot" button in the bottom right.

> CentOS Linux is now successfully installed and ready for you to use!
> Go ahead and reboot to start using it!
>
> [Reboot]

Now dismount the ISO image (if you don't you'll keep going through the install process) and shutdown the Virtual Machine.

Now we need to do some additional configuration to the Virtual Machine so that it can have both internet access and you can view the system from the browser later in the book.

With the Virtual Machine shutdown, click on "Settings". In the settings panel, click Network on the left. You will see that Adapter 1 is configured and attached to NAT. Let that setting as it is. Click on Adapter 2 and then check the "Enable Network Adapter" checkbox. In the "Attached to" dropdown, select "Host-only Adapter" and then ok.

Now click Start and once the boot is completed, you will see a command line prompt to login. We have finished the installation and initial configuration of CentOS.

```
CentOS Linux 7 (AltArch)
Kernel 3.10.0-327.el7.i686 on an i686

localhost login: _
```

Let's login and find out our ip address so that we can continue as if we had a VPS, which at this point we kind of do, but it is only available internally.

Find Your IP Address	
Command	ip addr
Result	System will display network information

After typing in *ip addr* and pressing enter, you will get a lot of information on the page. We are not concerned about the information after **1** (loopback connection), or **2,** but under **3**, there is an **inet** that may look similar to this: 192.168.1.50/24. Your ip address would be 192.168.1.50. All networks are different, but use that as a general guide.

Be sure to write this IP down. Chances are it is dynamic and may change overtime. If you think it might have changed be sure to reference back to the Find Your IP Address box above.

CHAPTER 4
60 SECOND DOCUMENTATION BOOTCAMP

In technology we live and die by the documentation that we produce. Imagine having a problem with a client's system and not knowing what it is running and what the IPs or password is. That is a common problem. It is typically not safe to store passwords anywhere, but you must come up with a method of securely storing this information. When you deal with large numbers of IPs and passwords, it is impossible to remember them all. Below is a helpful documentation guide to help get you started. Since this is for learning CentOS and not production, writing the password down is probably ok. If you are reading this digitally, then create a sheet of your own to place this information.

Example Data

Server Name: CentOS

Operating System: CentOS 7

Supported Till: 2024

Root Password: ********

IP Address: 000.000.000.000

Primary Purpose: Webserver

Date Installed: 6/20/2016

Last Date Updated: 6/20/2016

My Documentation

Server Name: _____

Operating System: CentOS 7

Supported Till: 2024

Root Password: _____

IP Address: _____

Primary Purpose: Webserver

Date Installed: _____

Last Date Updated: _____

Chapter 5

Getting to the CLI

CLI stands for command line interface, where you can interact with the system by entering lines of text. This is how we interact with our server.

If you decided not to use the recommended method of setting up a VPS, then you can see the CLI on your computers display. When you boot your computer, it will bring you to the CLI, where you can then login.

We can connect to the CentOS server by using a protocol called SSH. **SSH** stands for Secure Shell, which is an encrypted way that we can remote login to our server.

To prepare for the next steps, refer to the information that we documented in the last chapter as part of our documentation boot camp. We will need both the IP Address and login information. An **IP Address**, is a string of numbers that identifies a computer on a network. For our VPS, our IP Address is a public one, which can be accessed from anywhere with an internet connection. For a Virtual Machine, use the CLI interface that is displayed when you boot.

The program I recommend to SSH into your VPS server is called PuTTY. **PuTTY** is a free SSH client that is open source and supported on Windows. You can download it from the following link:

http://putty.org

The file you download is an executable (.exe) that does not require an install. Once you download it, you can drag it onto your desktop for quick access.

Connecting to your VPS or Virtual Machine with this tool is very easy. Under Host Name or IP address, put the IP address that was provided. Select SSH as the connection type and then click open. See figure 1 for an example of what it should look like.

Note: Your IP Address will be different than the one in the figure.

Figure 1: Putty Configuration

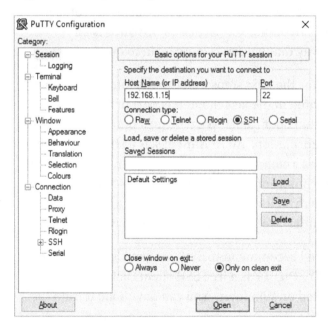

When you hit connect, you may get a message like the one in Figure 2. Click Yes.

Figure 2: PuTTY Security Alert

LOGGING IN FOR THE FIRST TIME

Now you will be prompted in for the first time. Enter the username root, then the password that was provided or set by you when setting up your VPS

If you used DigitalOcean, their system requires a password reset the first time you log in. You will need to reenter the provided password and then the new one you wish to set twice. Make sure you follow secure password guidelines and set a secure password for the root user.

Note: *Throughout this book, I use tables to explain the different commands that we are going to learn. The first row is the task that we want to do, the second is the command we need to use, and the third is an example of what your CLI will look like. I think this is the best way to depict and explain the commands we are going to learn.*

If you were not prompted to change your password, but want to, you can enter the command, *passwd*. See the table on the next page for more details.

Change My Password	
Command	passwd
Result	System will prompt for new password
CLI Display	[root@centos:~]# passwd Changing password for user root. New password: Retype new password: passwd: password updated successfully

When it prompts you for the new password, enter it and do not be concerned that the password does not appear on the screen. Once you have finished, press enter and type it one more time.

NAVIGATION

Do not be intimidated by the white text and black background on the CLI. I know that there is no mouse or graphics, but after a short while, you will be comfortable navigating through the directories on your server. **Directory** is like a folder that you may have used on a Windows or Mac device. As a person who has used this for a long time, I actually prefer this to having a graphical user interface. Before we do anything else, let's learn to explore the server. By using the *pwd* command, we can see the location of the directory that we are currently viewing.

Find Your Current Directory Location	
Command	pwd
Result	System will output the directory that you are in.
CLI Display	[root@centos:~]# pwd /root

Right now we are in a directory named root, which is essentially the home directory of the user root. **There is big difference between this root home directory and the actual root of the system.**

The path / is the root of the system, but right now we are in a subdirectory that is named root (/root).

The **root** of the server is the top directory. Everything is a subdirectory inside of it. From our current location, there are two ways we can go there. Let's start with the easiest command that will always get us to root.

Go To The Root Directory (/)	
Command	cd /
Result	We change to the main root directory
CLI Display	[root@centos:~]# cd / [root@centos:/]#

Now let's use, *pwd* again to see where we are at.

Find Your Current Directory Location	
Command	pwd
Result	System will output the directory that you are in.
CLI Display	[root@centos:~]# pwd /

If you want to see what is in the folder, we can use the ls command.

List Files	
Command	ls
Result	Lists the files in the current directory
CLI Display	[root@centos:/]# ls bin dev home media opt root sbin sys var boot etc lib mnt proc run srv tmp var

We can also go into more detail by adding a flag after *ls*.

A **flag** is typed at the prompt as part of our command and adds additional parameters to tell the system what we want.

Try running this command: *ls –la*

In that example, *–la* is the flag. The *l* tells the system that we want to see more details and *a* lists all the files in the directory, even the hidden ones.

Now, let's change to the directory named home.

Change Directory	
Command	cd home
Result	System moves us to child folder home
CLI Display	[root@centos:/]# cd home [root@centos: home]#

Note: It is important to understand the difference between parent and child directories. If we have a directory called documents and another inside of it called pictures. Pictures would be a child directory of documents. In this instance we were in the parent directory / and changed it to the child directory /home. If you were not in the parent folder, you could still navigate to home, but after cd, you would have to list the full path (example: cd /home) instead. If you get an error such as, "No such file or directory", you may need to enter the full path, since you may not be in the right parent directory.

If we want to go back to the root directory we can use another change directory command, which makes going up a directory very easy.

Move Up A Directory Level	
Command	cd ..
Result	System moves us to the parent folder
CLI Display	[root@centos: home]# cd .. [root@centos:/]#

Using *cd* along with the directory names and .. can allow us to quickly move throughout our server.

Quick Recap

1) **CLI** stands for command line interface, where you can interact with the system by entering lines of text.
2) **SSH** stands for Secure Shell, which is an encrypted way that we can remote login to our server.
3) An **IP Address**, is a string of numbers that identifies a computer on a network.
4) **PuTTY** is a free SSH client that is open source and supported on Windows.
5) The *passwd* command, allows us to change the current users password.
6) Entering *pwd*, will provide us with our current location in the server's directories.
7) Using *ls*, will list the files and directories in our current directory.
8) Adding a flag, such as *–la*, after *ls*, provides us with more details and shows hidden files.
9) We can use *cd*, to change directories quickly
    a. We can move up a folder with *cd ..*
    b. Putting a child directory after *cd,* will put us in the directory.
        i. Example: *cd home*
    c. We can always find root by using *cd /*
10) The path / is the root of the system, but /root is a child or sub directory named root.

Chapter 6

Creating a New User

The user 'root' has full access to the system. While we used it to learn some basic navigation, we should not use it as our main username for the system. It defeats the security model that is great and makes Linux systems so secure. By not using root, it also prevents accidental typo errors that could result in disasters. It's just good practice. What we will do in our next command is create a new user, named tidus, and then we will provide him with sudo access.

Sudo before a command, will allow our user, tidus, to be able to elevate it to higher security privileges to install software and make changes. Sudo runs the command as a super user, even though the user tidus would normally only have more limited access. This will come together soon, when we dive into using it, but first we need to create tidus's account.

Add a New User	
Command	adduser tidus
Result	System sets up user tidus
CLI Display	[root@centos:/]# adduser tidus [root@centos:/]#

Once you run that command, the system will add the user tidus. Next we need to set a password for this new user.

Earlier, we learned how to change our password. If you are root or a sudo user you can change a user's password as well by following the steps below.

Change a User's Password	
Command	passwd tidus
Result	System will prompt for you to set a new password for user tidus.
CLI Display	[root@centos:/]# passwd tidus New password: Retype new password: passwd: all tokens updated successfully

Ok, so now that we have tidus setup, we still need to grant him access to sudo. We would only do this for users that may need to increase their security privileges.

First we need to open the sudoer's configuration file to modify it. We can do this by using the visudo command.

Giving a User Sudo Privileges	
Command	visudo
Result	System will open the sudoer's file.
CLI Display	[root@centos:/]# visudo # This file MUST be edited with the 'visudo' command as root. # # ***Note: Arrow down the document*** # # #Allow root to run any commands anywh.. root ALL=(ALL) ALL ...

There is a lot of text in this file, but do not be intimidated. In the table above I arrowed down till I found the highlighted: **root   ALL=(ALL)   ALL**.

Below that selection we need to add the following:
tidus ALL=(ALL) ALL

In visudo, you are always in one of two modes: command or insert. Press I to insert text and ESC to goto command mode.

Press the down key until you are in the blank space under root. Once there type press *I* and type *tidus*, press tab, type *ALL=(ALL)*, press tab and type *ALL*. Now press the ESC key and type *:w* and then press enter to save. Next type *:q* and press enter to exit.

Now you can breathe. I know we dived in deep a little fast, but it is important that we start using a user id other than root. It is also important that at the same time we can install software and learn more, so this was needed.

Before we move on, we can learn two quick commands. Right now there is probably a lot of text on your CLI. If you want to clean that up, we can use the clear command.

Clearing the Screen	
Command	clear
Result	System will clear the screen
CLI Display	[root@centos:/]# clear

Now that we have a clear screen we can close out of PuTTY if you are using a VPS. If you are using a Virtual Machine type logout. We are going to continue on our new user id, tidus.

Logging Out	
Command	logout
Result	System will close SSH session and exit PuTTY or logout of a Virtual Machine
CLI Display	[root@centos:/]# logout

Quick Recap

1) We should avoid using the 'root' user as a good usage practice.
2) **sudo** before a command, allows a user to have super user privileges.
3) We can add a user by using the command *adduser*, with the username afterwards.
    a. Example: *adduser nathan*
4) We can change a user's password by using the *passwd* command before their name.
    a. Example: *passwd nathan*
5) To have access to use **sudo**, a user must first be added to the configuration file, which can be edited by using the *visudo* command.
6) If our CLI gets too cluttered, we can clear it by using the *clear* command.
7) To end our session and sign out, we can use *logout*.

Chapter 7

System Status at a Glance

Log into your server, with the new user that we created in the last chapter. From here, through the rest of the book, we will not be using the root user id.

Let's take a look at a few settings and see how our server is preforming.

First, we can take a look at our system uptime. This can be very useful in system administration. It lets you know how long the server has been online, how many users logged in, and the average system load.

Checking Uptime	
Command	uptime
Result	System will display the uptime and load average data
CLI Display	[tidus@centos:~]$ uptime

Next we can see what processes are using the most memory on our system by using the *top* command. This can be useful if your system is running sluggish to see what is hogging the system resources.

The first few lines will give you a summary of the resource utilization on your system and you can sort the list of processes by CPU or memory use, which allows you to quickly see where your server is receiving the biggest demands on its resources.

Checking System CPU Usage	
Command	top
Result	System will display processes using the most CPU resources
CLI Display	[tidus@centos:~]$ top

To exit *top*, press control and c.

To check the systems memory resources, we can use the *vmstat* command.

Checking Memory Usage	
Command	vmstat
Result	System will display the amount of memory free and in use
CLI Display	[tidus@centos:~]$ vmstat

Between *vmstat* and *top* as you become more skilled, you will be able to determine, which scripts or programs are maxing system resources if there is a problem. It is a good habit to keep an eye on these to just make sure usage is where it should be.

In a larger environment, you may want to see what users are logged into the server. Using the *w* command provides us with this information.

Checking Memory Usage	
Command	w
Result	System will display the users on the server
CLI Display	[tidus@centos:~]# w

NAVIGATING, MAKING DIRECTORIES, AND FILES

Some of this is going to recap earlier chapters, but this repetition is important to remembering the commands that you will be using frequently in daily usage.

Now that we have logged in, use the *pwd* command to see our current directory.

Find Your Current Directory Location	
Command	pwd
Result	System will output the directory that you are in.
CLI Display	[tidus@centos:~]$ pwd /home/tidus

Notice that our directory this time is different than it was when we logged in with the root user. Last time we were at /root, which was the home directory for root. This time we are at /home/tidus, which is the home directory for the user tidus.

Tip: If you ever need to get back to your home directory use *cd*, to get back to your users home folder.

Now that we are in our home folder, let's make a new directory called 'documents'.

Making a New Directory	
Command	mkdir documents
Result	System will create a child directory called documents
CLI Display	[tidus@centos:~]$ mkdir documents [tidus@centos:~]$

Use the *ls* command to list the contents of our home directory and see if the directory 'documents' is there.

List Files	
Command	ls
Result	Lists the files in the current directory
CLI Display	[tidus@centos:~]# ls documents

From using *ls*, we now see that our directory is empty outside of the directory 'documents'.

Let's use what we have learned from the previous chapters to practice our navigation skills and go into the documents directory.

Try using the command: *cd Documents*

You may notice that it returns, "cd: Documents: No such file or directory." Linux is case sensitive, which means that 'Documents' and 'documents' are two separate things. You will want to keep that in mind as you use CentOS, since using the correct case matters.

Now let's do it the right way.

Change to a Child Directory	
Command	cd documents
Result	Changes to the documents directory
CLI Display	[tidus@centos:~]$ cd documents [tidus@centos: documents]$

Use the *ls* command to list the files in the directory, you'll notice that it is empty.

Now let's go back home by using, *cd*.

Change to User Home Directory	
Command	cd
Result	Changes to user's home directory
CLI Display	[tidus@centos: documents]$ cd [tidus@centos:~]$

If we use *pwd* we will find that we are back at, /home/tidus.

Now, use *cd* with the full path to the documents directory. Remember, that Linux is case sensitive.

Change Directory Using a Full Path	
Command	cd /home/tidus/documents
Result	Changes to specified directory
CLI	[tidus@centos:~]$ cd /home/tidus/documents [tidus@centos: documents]$

If we wanted to get the parent directory of this folder we can also use: *cd ..*

Move Up A Directory Level	
Command	cd ..
Result	System moves us to the parent folder
CLI Display	[tidus@centos: documents]$ cd .. [tidus@centos:~]$

You should be getting the hang of it now!

Experiment some more and in the next section we will create some files using the built in text editor, nano.

CREATING AND EDITING FILES WITH NANO

Nano is a useful text editor for the command line interface (CLI) in Linux systems. Since we are using the CLI, nano is keyboard oriented with control keys, rather than using a mouse. By learning some of the control keys, you will be able to quickly edit files from the nano editor. Once you pick this up and learn more about using Linux by the command line you can then move onto more advanced editors like vi and, which are great, but often have a steeper learning curve.

Nano is easy to use and great for beginners. It is often installed by default in most VPS configurations of CentOS, but on a Virtual Machine you may need to install it. It's a WYSIWYG editor; "what you see is what you get."

We will talk about installing packages to CentOS more in a later chapter, but in case you do not have nano, you can install it by using the command and then typing your password when prompted: ***sudo yum install nano***

The CLI may also ask you for permission. If it does, press y and then enter.

Again, we will discuss installing packages in more detail later, but that command, if you don't already have nano, will install it to your server.

Let's go ahead and create a file using nano.

Creating a file in nano	
Command	nano notes.txt
Result	System launches nano for new file notes.txt
CLI Display	[tidus@centos:~]$ nano notes.txt

Now, you will notice that we are in a simple text editor. Since we do not have a mouse we can get a list of the control keys by pressing control and G at the same time.

See a complete list of nano command keys in the table below:

Nano command keys
^ represents the control 'Ctrl' key.   ^G (F1)   Display this help text   ^X (F2)   Exit from nano   ^O (F3)   Write the current file to disk   ^J (F4)   Justify the current paragraph   ^R (F5)   Insert another file into the current one   ^W (F6)   Search for a string or a regular expression   ^Y (F7)   Go to previous screen   ^V (F8)   Go to next screen

```
                Nano command keys (cont.)

^K    (F9)        Cut the current line and store it in the
cutbuffer
^U    (F10)       Uncut from into the current line
^C    (F11)       Display the position of the cursor
^T    (F12)       Invoke the spell checker, if available
M-\   (M-|)       Go to the first line of the file
M-/   (M-?)       Go to the last line of the file

^Y Prev Page      ^P Prev Line      ^X Exit
^V Next Page      ^N Next Line
```

In the nano editor, enter the following text:

Nano notes: Nano is a useful text editor for the command line interface (CLI) in Linux systems. Since we are using the CLI, nano is keyboard oriented with control keys, rather than using a mouse.

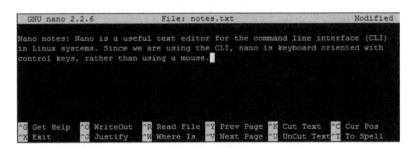

Once you have the text entered, use the exit command keys:

Control + X

You then will be prompted if you want to "Save modified buffer?" Press Y then Enter to save the file.

Now let's see what is in our folder by using the *ls* command.

List Files	
Command	ls
Result	Lists the files in the current directory
CLI Display	[tidus@centos:~]$ ls documents notes.txt

Editing, Deleting, Moving, and Copying

With our notes.txt file created, we can now learn how to move, edit, delete, and copy files.

To get started, let's copy the notes.txt file to a new file called test.txt. To do this we will use the *cp* command, which will allow us to copy one file to another. To use *cp*, we need to also provide the file we want to copy, and also the file we want to copy into. See the table below:

Copy to New File	
Command	cp notes.txt test.txt
Result	System copies notes.txt and creates a new file, test.txt with the contents.
CLI Display	[tidus@centos:~]$ cp notes.txt test.txt [tidus@centos:~]$

By using the *ls* command, we can check to see if the file was copied.

List Files	
Command	ls
Result	Lists the files in the current directory
CLI Display	[tidus@centos:~]$ls documents notes.txt test.txt

Now that we have two files, we should open test.txt in nano and make a few changes.

Open a File in Nano	
Command	nano test.txt
Result	System will open test.txt in nano.
CLI Display	[tidus@centos:~]$ nano test.txt

When you open the file, you will notice that it has the same text as our notes.txt file. To the beginning of this document, let's add a line: *This document is a test for learning Linux.*

Once that is added. Save the file as we did earlier.

With the *cp* command, the file is copied. When we move a file, it is like using cut in Windows as the original is deleted.

We will now move test.txt into the documents directory. By using the *mv* command we can move files. After *mv*, we put the name of the file we want to move and then the location we want to move it to.

Move a File	
Command	mv test.txt documents/test.txt
Result	System will open test.txt in nano.
CLI Display	[tidus@centos:~]$ mv test.txt documents/test.txt [tidus@centos:~]$

If you change your directory to documents and use *ls* you will find the test.txt file is now located there.

Change Directory to Documents and List Files	
Command	cd documents; ls
Result	System will change to documents and list files.
CLI Display	[tidus@centos:~]$ cd documents; ls [tidus@centos: documents]$ test.txt

You may notice above that I used a semi-colon after *cd documents*. This allows us to combine two commands. In this example the semi-colon allowed us to change directory and then list the files in the new directory.

Now we can also use *mv* to rename a file. Using the command below, we can rename the file and list the files in the directory.

Using mv to Change File Name	
Command	mv test.txt newtest.txt; ls
Result	System will change the file name to newtest.txt and list the files in the directory.
CLI Display	[tidus@centos: documents]$ mv test.txt newtest.txt; ls newtest.txt

Hopefully you are not too attached to this file as in the next table, we will learn how to delete a file, using *rm*.

Using rm to Delete a File	
Command	rm newtest.txt
Result	System will delete newtest.txt
CLI Display	[tidus@centos: documents]$ rm newtest.txt [tidus@centos: documents]$

If want you can use *ls*, but you will find that the directory is empty.

Now let's go back to our parent directory.

Move to Parent Directory	
Command	cd ..
Result	System will move up to parent directory
CLI Display	[tidus@centos: documents]$ cd .. [tidus@centos:~]$

When deleting files or directories, be very careful as one misstep could delete the entire system. Avoiding using the root user helps with this.

Sometimes you may want to delete a directory, but to delete a directory we must add a flag.

If we use *rm documents*, we will get an error that it is a directory.

To delete a directory, we must use the command in the table below.

Delete a Directory	
Command	rm –r documents
Result	System will delete the directory named documents.
CLI Display	[tidus@centos:~]$ rm –r documents [tidus@centos:~]$

To delete a directory, we have to use the *–r* flag.

Chapter 8

Updating The Server

In the last few chapters, we got a foundation in navigation and managing files. Another thing that is vital to a strong foundation is knowing how to update your server.

As we install updates and packages, we will be using a utility called **yum**. YUM stands for Yellowdog Updater Modified and is an open source CLI package management tool. It allows users to easily install, update, remove or search software packages on some Linux systems like CentOS.

For us to update the server, we will need to give tidus super user privileges. In the first yum command below, we will update the list of packages and get information on the newest versions.

Update Package Information	
Command	sudo yum update
Result	System will increase the user's rights, search for an updated list of packages, and look for newer versions.
CLI Display	[tidus@centos:~]$ sudo yum update password for tidus:

After you run that, your CLI will list a long list of web addresses as it checks the various package lists for updates. It may ask you if you wish to continue and if it does type *y* and press enter.

With the new information of updates that are available, we can now upgrade our server to have the latest versions of the current packages. Using the command below will fetch the new versions and install them onto the server.

	Upgrade Server Packages
Command	sudo yum upgrade
Result	System will increase the user's rights, search for an updated list of packages, and look for newer versions.
CLI Display	[tidus@centos:~]$ sudo yum upgrade password for tidus: Do you want to continue? [Y/n] y [tidus@centos:~]$

After entering, Y to continue, the server will setup and install all of the newest versions of packages to our server.

Keeping your server with the latest updates installed is a vital foundation to a core level of security. There is much more you will need to learn to secure your system, but this is a basic step to get started.

Chapter 9

Setting Up a Web Server

Apache2

A common configuration for Linux servers is to set them up to be web servers. 80% of servers that host websites are running Linux. To establish a good foundation, learning how to install these features are important.

To get started in setting this server up as a web server, we need to install Apache2. Apache2 is the most commonly used web server on Linux systems. Web servers are used to serve up web pages requested by client computers. To run website software like WordPress we will need more packages than this, but installing Apache2 is the best starting place.

Installing Apache2	
Command	sudo yum install httpd
Result	System will install apache2 and dependent packages to the server.
CLI Display	[tidus@centos:~]$ sudo yum install httpd password for tidus: Do you want to continue? [Y/n] y [tidus@centos:~]$

Now, we should make a basic HTML file to test our webserver. In the CLI type the following command:

sudo nano /var/www/html/index.html

Inside of nano type: `<h1>It Works</h1>`

Then press control and x, then y to save and enter.

The <h1></h1>, if you are not familiar is an HTML tag for a header. It will make the text display big and bold at the top of the page.

Later in this book we will cover changing permissions, but for now use the following command to make the test HTML file viewable:

sudo chmod –R 755 /var/www/html/

That command is setting recursively the permissions to the html folder. More on that later.

We must start the Apache2 service so that the web service is running to make the page visible.

Starting Apache2	
Command	sudo service httpd start
Result	System will start apache2
CLI Display	[tidus@centos:~]$ sudo service httpd start password for tidus: [tidus@centos:~]$

You can now enter your ip address into any browser and see our test HTML file.

In the browser you should see: **It Works**

Reminder, if you use a Virtual Machine instead of a VPS, you will only be able to see this on your host computer's browser.

Stopping and Restarting Apache2

There may be an instance when you want to stop or restart the Apache2 webserver.

You can do so by using the following commands:

Stop Apache2: sudo service httpd stop

Start Apache2: sudo service httpd start

Restart Apache2: sudo service httpd restart

By default, your CentOS server will not start Apache2 at boot, which could be a problem if there is a power failure. Use the following command to have it start by default at boot:

```
sudo systemctl enable httpd.service
```

THE WEB FOLDER

You may be wondering, where are my website files located? On most CentOS installs you can get to the web directory by changing directory to /var/www/html.

Go To The HTML Directory	
Command	cd /var/www/html; ls
Result	System will change to the html directory and list the files.
CLI Display	[tidus@centos:~]$ cd /var/www/html index.html

If you want to, you can open the default index.html file in nano.

Open index.html in nano	
Command	nano index.html
Result	System will load index.html into nano.

Note: To save and make changes, you may need to open the file using sudo.

Now let's change back to our home directory by using *cd*.

INSTALLING MYSQL/MARIADB DATABASE

Along with Apache2 and PHP, your server will need MySQL for many web applications that need to store data. This includes the widely popular WordPress CMS. Recently, CentOS has removed MySQL and set MariaDB as the default database package. This will do the job for us as well.

\	Installing MariaDB Server
Command	sudo yum install mariadb-server
Result	System will install MariaDB Server

Like Apache2, we need to enter a command for MariaDB to start on system boot. Enter the following:

```
sudo systemctl enable mariadb.service
```

There may be an instance when you want to stop or restart the MariaDB database.

You can do so by using the following commands, which are similar to Apache2's commands:

Stop MariaDB: sudo service mariadb stop

Start MariaDB: sudo service mariadb start

Restart MariaDB: sudo service mariadb restart

Now that we have our database system running, we need to run a security script to remove some default settings that can be dangerous.

\multicolumn{2}{c}{Securing MariaDB Server}	
Command	sudo mysql_secure_installation
Result	System will prompt you for current password for the database server. One is not yet set so press enter. Then press Y to set a password and follow the on screen instructions.

INSTALLING PHP5

PHP is a popular web server-side scripting language. It is very popular and used by most content management systems, such as WordPress. It can display dynamic content, run scripts, connect to the database, and send information to the webserver.

\multicolumn{2}{c}{Installing PHP5}	
Command	sudo yum install php php-mysql
Result	System will install php5 and dependencies, along with the mysql package to talk to the database.
CLI Display	[tidus@centos:~]$ sudo yum install php php-mysql password for tidus: Is this ok? [Y/n] y [tidus@centos:~]$

For the changes to take effect, we need to restart Apache. Remember the command we learned earlier:

```
sudo service httpd restart
```

Now to test the install, we should make another test page using nano.

Enter the following:

```
sudo nano /var/www/html/php.php
```

Inside of nano, enter the following PHP code and save:

```
<?php phpinfo(); ?>
```

If you do not know PHP that is fine. This code just provides us with a sample page to ensure PHP is working.

Now, in your web browser enter the following:

http://myipaddress/php.php

Where I have myipaddress, you should replace that with your servers IP.

You should see a blueish looking table with various information about your PHP and system settings.

Before we move to the next part of the book, delete the index.html file and the php.php file. Remember to use the *rm* command and the files address such as:

rm /var/www/html/index.html

INSTALLING SENDMAIL

If you would like your website or server to be able to send mail, then installing Sendmail will help with that. Sendmail is a general email routing service that supports many mail transfer methods across the internet.

Installing Sendmail	
Command	sudo yum install sendmail
Result	System will install sendmail
CLI Display	[tidus@centos:~]$ sudo yum install sendmail password for tidus: Is this ok? [Y/n] y [tidus@centos:~]$

After you approve the install it will automatically finish the installation process.

Now we have the LAMP stack and sendmail installed! We won't cover the other various configuration settings in this book, but you can find various helpful resources online.

Chapter 10

Management Via The Browser

There are many circumstances where you may wish to see server information or manage some things through the web browser. Often times for new users this is easier than the CLI. Users that master the CLI, will likely prefer to use it over a graphical management interface.

Webmin is a web-based tool for Linux and Unix systems. It allows users to manage users, disk settings, the network, firewall, Apache, DNS, and many other items inside of a graphical interface.

The next steps will walk you through installing this tool.

To begin, we need to add the webmin repository information to CentOS. To do so enter the following command:

```
sudo nano /etc/yum.repos.d/webmin.repo
```

Then inside of nano enter the following:

```
[Webmin]
name=Webmin Distribution Neutral
#baseurl=http://download.webmin.com/download/yum
mirrorlist=http://download.webmin.com/download/yum/mirrorlist
enabled=1
```

Save the file and then enter the following two commands:

```
sudo yum check-update
```

```
rpm --import http://www.webmin.com/jcameron-key.asc
```

Now that yum is updated, we can run the install.

```
sudo yum install webmin -y
```

When the install completes, run the two commands below to start the service and have it run automatically on boot:

```
sudo chkconfig webmin on
```

```
sudo service webmin start
```

By default webmin can be accessed by going to:

```
http://myipaddress:10000
```

If that does not prompt you to login, enter the following command in the CLI to open up the port on your systems firewall:

```
firewall-cmd -add-port=10000/tcp
```

If you choose to use webmin, there is a lot of documentation and resource on how to use it at:

```
http://doxfer.webmin.com/Webmin/Main_Page
```

Use that link as your resource to using this platform if you choose to manage the server via this resource.

Chapter 11

Understanding Permissions

To understand how to allocate permissions to users and groups, we must first understand how the Linux permissions work. It is much easier than determining Window's Server permissions, once you establish an understanding for it.

On a Window's Server there are a variety of permission types to allocate. See the figure below:

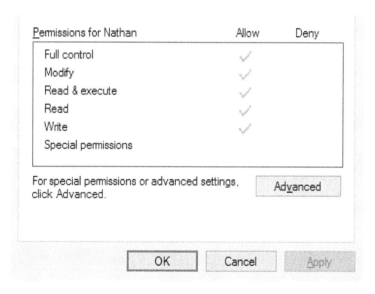

CentOS and other Linux systems have three basic permission groups and three basic permission types.

Permission Groups

Owner – The owner permissions apply only to the owner of the file or directory.

Group – The group permissions apply only to the group that has been assigned to the file or directory.

All Users – The all user's permissions apply to all users on the system. This is the permission group you will want to be the most careful of.

Permission Types

Read – The read permission refers to a user's capability to read the contents of the file, but does not allow them to write or save changes.

Write – The write permissions refer to a user's capability to write or modify a file or directory.

Execute – The execute permission affects a user's capability to execute a file or view the contents of a directory.

We can view the existing permissions and check them by using the CLI and our familiar *ls* command, with the *–l* flag.

Example to List Files with Details	
Command	ls -l
Result	Lists the files in the current directory with details
CLI Display	[tidus@centos:~]$ ls –l -rw-rw-r-- 1 tidus tidus 196 Feb 13 20:48 notes.txt

Dissecting the output:
-rw-rw-r-- 1 tidus tidus 196 Feb 13 20:48 notes.txt

The first section that is displayed, -rw-rw-r--, shows the permissions for the file.

When we are viewing the permissions by using the *ls –l* command, we can understand them by using the following key.

Understanding File Permissions	
Read	r
Write	w
Execute	x

As we view the permission for our notes.txt file, we can make a few observations based on the output: -rw-rw-r--.

The first three characters –rw, tells us that the user tidus has read and write permissions for the file notes.txt. The second set of characters shows us that the group tidus, also has read and write permissions. The last, shows us the all users permissions. From looking at the output, all users can read the file, but not write to it.

USING BINARY REFERENCES TO SET PERMISSIONS

Noe what we understand the basics of permission groups and permission types, setting permissions using binary references, should be fairly simple. It is important to understand that when you set file permissions this way, it is done by three integers. An **integer** is a whole number (Example: 1, 2, and 4).

To set permissions, we must determine the binary representation of the *rwx* string. **RWX String** is the binary representation that allows us to set read, write, and execute permissions.

We must use the table below to calculate the permissions we want for a file or directory.

File Permissions: Binary Representation	
Read	4
Write	2
Execute	1

We get the permission number by adding the integers together. We must do this for each of the three permission groups.

For example:

Read Access = 4

Read and Write Access = 6

Read, Write, and Execute Permission = 7

Each permission group needs a number. The number we make for setting permissions will be 3 digits. Remember, the order is user, group, and all users.

Exercise 1: What does a permission of 777 mean?

This means that the user, group, and all users have read, write, and execute access. Using 777 as a permission setting is not good for establishing strong security.

Exercise 2: What does a permission of 655 mean?

This means that the user has permission to read and write. The group has permission to read and execute. All users can also read and execute.

Exercise 3: What does a permission of 444 mean?

This means that both the user, group, and all users have only read access to a file.

Exercise 4: What does a permission of 755 mean?

This means that the user has read, write, and execute permission. The group and all users can only read and execute. This is often the permission setting recommended for the web directory for those using WordPress.

Before we go over the steps of applying permissions we should first learn how to transfer files. That process will open the door for applications in which we will learn to set permissions.

OVERVIEW: OWNERSHIP OF FILES AND DIRECTORIES

In the next few pages in this book we will provide a few examples for tidus to change permissions of files and directories. When you are ready, let's create some sample files and directories. With the commands we learned earlier.

Make a folder called 'files' in tidus's home directory:

```
mkdir /home/tidus/files
```

Make a file named 'test.txt' with nano:

```
nano /home/tidus/files/test.txt
```

Inside of nano, you may enter whatever you wish for this exercise.

tidus already owns the directory files, but if he didn't, you could use the following command. You will notice the –R flag being used. This means that the ownership applies to all files and sub directories.

	Changing the Owner of a Directory
Command	sudo chown tidus -R /home/tidus/files
Result	System will make tidus the owner of the directory, along with all subdirectories.
CLI Display	[tidus@centos:~]$ sudo chown tidus -R /var/www password for tidus: [tidus@centos:~]$

To review the command above we must note that we need to use *sudo*. This elevates the permissions for tidus. Without the use of *sudo*, we will get errors and the command will fail.

After *sudo*, we use *chown* which allows us to change the owner of the directory. The command *chown*, requires a user (tidus) and a directory (/home/tidus/files). The flag –R will make tidus the owner of all the subdirectories as well. By using this, tidus also owns the directory named files.

Alternativley, we chould change the owner of the file we created (test.txt). There is no need to execute this, since tidus is already an owner, but experiment with this overtime to practice.

	Changing the Owner of a File
Command	sudo chown tidus /home/tidus/test.txt
Result	System will make tidus the owner of the file.

Chapter 12

Adding a Database to MariaDB

In other books I have written about Linux, I had users use a web tool called phpmyadmin to add users and databases. In this book, I want to take a different approach and do this from the command line interface.

As we progress into installing WordPress, it will need a database to store its information into. In these next steps, we will create that database and a user to connect to that database.

To begin, we must login to MariaDB's root account by using the following command:

```
sudo mysql -u root -p
```

As you may have guessed, the *u* flag symbolizes user and *p* stands for password.

You will be prompted to enter the root password for MariaDB. You would have set this when we ran the command to secure the install.

Once you are logged in, the next step is to create the database. We are going to name this database 'wordpress'.

```
CREATE DATABASE wordpress;
```

Please note that capitals do matter here as they do for other commands. Additionally all MySQL and MariaSQL statements must end with a semi-colon.

That was easy! Now we need to create a new user account that will only be able to operate with the database we created. This allows for good security and better control of database permissions.

For me, I am going to call the new user account 'wpuser'. In the command below, you can use a different name if you wish and change 'password' to a secure password. We will need this password as we connect WordPress to the database.

```
CREATE USER wpuser@localhost IDENTIFIED BY 'password';
```

Right now you have a database and user account, but the user account cannot yet access the wordpress database. We need to grant that user access to the wordpress database with the following command.

```
GRANT ALL PRIVLEGES ON wordpress.* TO wpuser@localhost IDENTIFIED BY 'password';
```

Our user now has access to the database, but we need to do something called flush so that MySQL/MariaDB knows about the privilege changes we made. Use the following command:

```
FLUSH PRIVLEGES;
```

Now that we have done these commands, we can exit MySQL/MariaDB by using the following command:

```
exit
```

Easy right? There is much more to learn about using MySQL and MariaDB. I recommend you continue expanding your knowledge on these topics as they are a very in demand skillset.

Chapter 13

Preparing For And Installing WordPress

There are a lot of different content management systems and platforms that you can install. Nearly 25% of all websites online are using WordPress as reported in 2015. This makes it one of the most widely used platforms. In addition to being very popular, there is a lot we can learn by installing this on our server for future reference as you roll out sites with other systems. We already know how to make a database and user so now we need to know how to install a package like this.

Before we can install WordPress, there are a few packages you may need to install depending on your VPS or Virtual Machine install. Use the following to ensure that you have the proper configuration.

The first thing we need to load is php-gd. This is needed for WordPress and other platforms to resize thumbnail images properly. We can install this with the following command:

```
sudo yum install php-gd
```

Be sure to enter your password and press y when prompted.

So that Apache can see the new module, we will need to restart httpd.

```
sudo service httpd restart
```

Now there are a few more packages we need. The first is wget. Wget is a program that gathers content from webservers. It allows us to download files from the web to our server. To install wget, use the following command:

```
sudo yum install wget
```

Again, be sure to enter your password and press y when prompted.

The next tool we will need to streamline the process is called rsync. Rsync is a utility that allows us to keep copies of files on the computer system and synchronize files to other folders. To install rsync, use the following command:

```
sudo yum install rsync
```

DOWNLOADING WORDPRESS

One of the reasons that I like WordPress for my tutorials is that it is easy to configure for new users and the team at WordPress always keeps the most stable version of their software at the same link.

Before we continue, make sure that you are in your home directory. Remember that you can get home at any time by entering *cd* into the CLI.

Now that we are sure that we are in the home directory, we can use wget to get the most resent version of WordPress with the following command:

```
cd wget http://wordpress.org/latest.tar.gz
```

This downloads a compressed version of WordPress that we will now need to extract using the tar command. In Linux, tar stands for tape archive from back in the day when most system administrators would backup files to tape backup drives. For our purpose will allow us to gather the compressed files from the download and extract them to our home directory. We can do that with the following command:

```
tar xzvf latest.tar.gz
```

Inside of your home folder, you will now have a directory called wordpress. To finish the installation, we need to move the files to the Apache document root (/var/www/html). Using the handy rsync tool, this is very easy. Use the following command to sync the files over to the Apache directory.

```
sudo rsync -avP ~/wordpress/ /var/www/html/
```

Remember, capitalization is important. One small error in this command could cause an issue for you moving forward. After the command is run, rsync will do the work and copy all of the files into the /var/www/html directory.

We still have one thing to do, we need to make an uploads folder for WordPress to store files. Using the mkdir command as we did earlier, makes this easy.

```
sudo mkdir /var/www/html/wp-content/uploads
```

Recap on Changing Ownership and Permissions and Editing Files

Now we have two more steps to finish a proper configuration. We need to change the ownership permissions to the WordPress files and folders. This will increase security and allow WordPress to function as expected. To do this, we will use the chown command as explained earlier in the book.

```
sudo chown -R apache:apache /var/www/html/*
```

Changing the Owner of Apache Web Directory	
Command	sudo chown –R apache:apache /var/www/html/*
Result	System will change ownership to apache for the /var/www/html director and sub-directories
CLI Display	[tidus@centos:~]$ sudo chown –R apache:apache /var/www/html/* password for tidus: [tidus@centos:~]$

Now our last step is the configuration the WordPress file that will connect us to the database we made. Make sure you remember the database name, user name, and password that we set.

First, we need to change to the /var/www/html directory.

Changing Directory	
Command	cd /var/www/html
Result	System will move us into the html directory
CLI Display	[tidus@centos:~]$ cd /var/www/html [tidus@centos: html]$

WordPress uses a file called wp-config.php to connect to the database. In the install, a sample file is provided. We need to copy that file and configure it with our database settings.

Copy File	
Command	sudo cp wp-config-sample.php wp-config.php
Result	System will copy the file into a new one with the required file name.
CLI Display	[tidus@centos: html]$ sudo cp wp-config-sample.php wp-config.php [tidus@centos: html]$

Now that we have a configuration file we can modify, we can edit it using nano.

```
sudo nano wp-config.php
```

The only modifications that we need to make inside of this file for our database connection is to the following fields: DB_NAME, DB_USER, and DB_PASSWORD. This will allow the website to talk to the database. Look at the following page for the example of my configuration.

Note: You should not use password as a password and is only used in this book as a guide.

WP-Config.php Configuration
| ```
/** The name of the database for WordPress */
define('DB_NAME', 'wordpress');

/** MySQL database username */
define('DB_USER', 'wpuser');

/** MySQL database password */
define('DB_PASSWORD', 'password');
``` |

Those are the only values that you should change inside of that file. When you are done, close and save the changes from nano.

ACCESSING WORDPRESS VIA THE BROWSER

The final steps that we need to do in this is to access WordPress from our browser. To do this, enter your ip address (http://myipaddress) into the browser. You should see a screen like the one on the following page.
```

Welcome

Welcome to the famous five-minute WordPress installation process! Just fill in the information below and you'll be on your way to using the most extendable and powerful personal publishing platform in the world.

Information needed

Please provide the following information. Don't worry, you can always change these settings later.

Site Title

Username

Usernames can have only alphanumeric characters, spaces, underscores, hyphens, periods and the @ symbol.

Password, twice

A password will be automatically generated for you if you leave this blank.

Strength indicator

Hint: The password should be at least seven characters long. To make it stronger, use upper and lower case letters, numbers, and symbols like ! " ? $ % ^ &).

Your E-mail

Double-check your email address before continuing.

Privacy

☑ Allow search engines to index this site.

[Install WordPress]

Complete the requested information for the site and then click on the 'Install WordPress' button. This will confirm the install and create the tables inside of the database automatically for you.

To continue hit the 'Login' button at the bottom of the page.

Now you have a working WordPress system up and running on your CentOS server.

Chapter 14

Final Remarks

Congratulations! In just under 85 pages we have established some CentOS 7 basics and used that information to build a basic webserver.

There much more to learn of course, but this is just the beginning. This guide should have you comfortable with navigating and installing packages on CentOS 7 as you move forward in experimentation and learning. Hopefully now using the command line interface is a little less scary.

If you have any questions for further learning, do not hesitate to email me at info@nathanneil.com.

Thank you and good luck as you continue learning!

CPSIA information can be obtained
at www.ICGtesting.com
Printed in the USA
BVHW040812071119
563167BV00008B/61/P